Published in the United States of America by Hallmark Cards, Inc.

ISBN: 0-87529-639-4

Printed in the United States of America.

The journey of a thousand miles begins with a broken fan belt and a leaky tire.

5

Do not walk behind me,
 for I may not lead.
Do not walk ahead of me,
 for I may not follow.
Do not walk beside me, either,
 Just leave me alone.

If you don't like my driving, don't call anyone. Just take another road. That's why the highway department made so many of them.

My performance at work has really improved over the years. Now I can nail a moving coworker with a paper clip shot from a rubber band at 20 yards.

13

My new low-fat diet is really working! The fat seems to hang lower every day.
maxine

I don't mind when tourists use
my varicose veins as a road map.
It's when they try to fold my leg
and put it in the glove compartment
that I get steamed.

When I'm feeling down,
    I like to whistle.
It makes the neighbor's dog
run to the end of his chain
    and gag himself.

18

No matter how bad things get, there's always something you can do: whine, moan and complain.

Never look a gift horse
   in the mouth,
      and don't get
        too close to
          the other end, either.

It's always darkest just before the dawn. So if you're going to steal the neighbor's newspaper, that's the time to do it.

A handy telephone tip:
Keep a small chalkboard near your phone. That way, when a salesman calls, you can hold the receiver up to it and run your fingernails across it until he hangs up.

Each day I try to enjoy
something from each
of the four food groups,
The bonbon group,
The salty-snack group,
The caffeine group,
        and
"whatever-the-thing-
in-the-tinfoil-in
the-back-of-
the-fridge-is" group.

Ah, the thrill of modern dance!

The sweeping musical majesty,
the joy of poetic motion,
the challenge of stuffing
a dollar bill into
a bouncing bikini brief...

How much of a tip to leave in a restaurant is always a controversial question. I usually recommend half a crouton, or for exceptional service, throw in that little sprig of parsley.

33

Nothing in the world is quite so fun as pouring old milk into new containers before having guests over!

35

I work as hard as the next guy!

Provided the next guy is a lazy relative of the boss who's riding the gravy train to retirement.

When you find yourself getting irritated with someone, try to remember that all men are brothers... and just give them a noogie or an Indian burn.

If genius is one percent inspiration and 99 percent perspiration, I wind up sharing elevators with a lot of bright people.

Floyd

38

Men are like small children... you bring a new one home, and the ones already there resent it.

Floyd

40

I always say, "The bigger they are, the harder it is to find jeans to fit over them."

42

They say you can't really know someone until you walk a mile in their shoes. I say if they've got itsy-bitsy feet or some kinda foot disease, I don't wanna know 'em!

Floyd

A man's best friend is his dog.

That's assuming you want a friend who messes on your carpet and drools on your newspaper.

If they lined up all
the men in the World...

... it would be
one goofy line.

If I won the lottery, I wouldn't be one of those people who immediately quit their jobs.

I'd make my boss's life a living hell for a week or two first.

I'd love to meet a man who has a really good head on his shoulders... and not just a bunch of loose hairs.

49

51

52

Last night I was in the mood to see something silly and idiotic on TV.

So I put the cat there.

Reach for the stars!
(It keeps your chest from sagging.)

People who live in glass houses shouldn't cavort nude on top of the piano doing gorilla impersonations.

A rose by any
other name
would stick
you just as bad
and
draw just as much
blood when you
grab a thorn.

You can't teach an old dog new tricks. But if you just teach him to stay out of my yard, that's enough!

If I wanted to hear the pitter-patter of little feet, I'd put shoes on my cat.

Ahh! the joys of cable!
Live sports, top-rated movies,
and best of all, flashes of
about four inches of
underwear while the
installer bends
over the set.

You can't judge a book by its cover.

You have to read the underlined parts to tell if it's any good.

Love is like
a roller coaster:
when it's good
you don't want
to get off,
and when
it isn't...

... you can't wait
to throw up.

WRITTEN BY: Chris Brethwaite, Bill Bridgeman, Bill Gray, Allyson Jones, Kevin Kinzer, Mark Oatman, Scott Oppenheimer, Dan Taylor, Rich Warwick and Myra Zirkle.

Books from:

SHOEBOX GREETINGS

(A tiny little division of Hallmark)

STILL MARRIED AFTER ALL THESE YEARS
DON'T WORRY, BE CRABBY: Maxine's Guide to Life
40: THE YEAR OF NAPPING DANGEROUSLY
THE MOM DICTIONARY
THE DAD DICTIONARY
WORKIN' NOON TO FIVE: The Official Workplace Quiz Book
WHAT... ME, 30?
THE FISHING DICTIONARY
YOU EXPECT ME TO SWALLOW THAT? The Official Hospital Quiz Book
THE GOOD, THE PLAID AND THE BOGEY: A Glossary of Golfing Terms
THE CHINA PATTERN SYNDROME: Your Wedding and How to Survive It
THE GRANDPARENT DICTIONARY
STILL A BABE AFTER ALL THESE YEARS?
CRABBY ROAD: More Thoughts on Life From Maxine
THE HANDYMAN DICTIONARY A Guide For the Home Mess-It-Up-Yourselfer